Ma

Visiting
Moissac Abbey

Photographs by Jean-Paul Gisserot
and Guy-Marie Renié

Translated by Angela Moyon

ÉDITIONS SUD OUEST

The minster flanks the north side of Place Roger-Delthil, laid out as a regular square in the 18th century. The carved main entrance, an integral part of the westwork at the western end of the church, faces the town. To the right, in the nave, bricks mark the 15th-century reconstruction work. (Photo by Jean-Paul Gisserot)

It is easy to imagine the prestige of an abbey such as Moissac, founded by Clovis I (481-511) whose conversion had ensured the triumph of Roman Catholicism in Gaul. Shortly after the victorious outcome to the Battle of Vouillé when the king's troops defeated the Arian Visigoths, it is said that the King of the Franks had a vision which inspired him to commission the building of a monastery for one thousand monks, at the confluence of the Tarn and Garonne rivers. Although numerous texts recall the royal origins of the abbey, this is doubtless a legend invented by the monks before the 11th century.

Did the legend contain anything of historic truth? Modern critics tend to attribute the founding of the abbey to Dagobert's son, Clovis II (635-657 A.D), King of Neustria and Burgundy. The least uncertain of the sources, St. Didier of Cahors' Vita, states that the monastery was founded during the episcopacy of Didier (630-655 A.D) and that it received generous royal gifts.

The location was not totally deserted when the new religious community settled here. A Gallo-Roman hypocaust which heated one of the rooms in Roman baths has been uncovered beneath St. Martin's Church (for the benefit of visitors, it should be specified that this small church on the Agen road just on the outskirts of Moissac is not open to the public but that, from the outside, it is possible to see the work carried out in the 6th or 7th centuries then, later, in the 10th, 13th, 14th, 15th and 17th centuries). However, nothing significant has been found on the site of the abbey itself, the building which undoubtedly led to the development of the town.

In 680 A.D, half a century after its founding, the abbey saw a marked upturn in its fortunes thanks to donations from rich property owners, Nizezius and his wife, Ermintrude, who gave it some thirty thousand hectares of land i.e. eighteen villae in the Garonne Valley with all the churches, lands, mills, serfs, settlers and freemen thereon.

Since subsequent documentary evidence is missing, the abbey's history then blurs into the history of Aquitaine, which suffered invasion at the hands of the Saracen, Normans and Magyars. However, it is known that, at the beginning of the 11th century, Louis the Pious visited the monastery and granted it his protection, thereby continuing the policy instigated by his predecessors.

The cloister and galleries were a westernised architectural version of the «enclosure» in monastic communities. The vast garth was built here on the north side of the church in order to make use of a spring which supplied water to the fountain in the cloister. The galleries were passageways or places of meditation and procession; they linked the church to the other abbey buildings. (Photo by Guy-Marie Renié)

All that remains of the Carolingian church is the altar discovered in 1963 beneath the pavement in the chancel.

In the 11th century the abbey was on the brink of financial ruin and, as a result of a weakening of royal power, it fell under the authority of a secular abbot who was supposed to ensure its protection. In 1030, part of the church collapsed. In 1042, the Viscount of Lomagne set fire to the monastic buildings. The Count of Toulouse and Bishop of Cahors then asked for the abbey to be annexed to Cluny, giving one of the most active centres of monastic revival a stepping stone from which to expand into Spain.

In 1048, Durand de Bredons, a close friend of Abbot Odilon of Cluny, became Abbot of Moissac. Religious reform was accompanied by the recovery of the monastery's property and privileges, which were further strengthened by Cluniac immunities. Spiritual and material revival soon led to new building projects. A new church, shown by archaeological digs to have been of the same size as the building we see today, was consecrated amid great pomp and ceremony in 1063; the cloister was finished in 1100. The library was enlarged by the inclusion of books copied in the scriptorium.

Hugely influential abbots succeeded each other at the head of the monastery – Durand de Bredons (1048-1072) who was also Bishop of Toulouse from 1060, Hunaud de Gavaret (1072-1085) then Ansquitil (1085-1115) and Roger (1115-1135) to whom we owe the cloister and entrance. Moissac was then in its heyday. The prosperity continued until the mid 14th century, and the monastic buildings were rebuilt by Bertrand de Montaigut (1260-1295).

After the Hundred Years' War, the abbey enjoyed a period of revival reflected in the reconstruction of the church. Yet the decline continued. In 1466, Moissac was separated from Cluny. The system of commendatory abbots placed at its head influential men who took the income but paid little heed to the need for management. In 1626, the abbey was secularised and the minster became a collegiate church.

The French Revolution confirmed the disappearance of the religious community. The buildings were sold off as national property or used for other purposes. In 1840 a new era dawned for the abbey. It had become a listed building and was acknowledged to be a particularly fine example of Romanesque architecture. There was no radical work but, instead, on-going restoration, conservation and enhancement which is still continuing today.

The abbey site

The abbey lies at the foot of the hills overlooking the valley, at the entrance to a small dale containing a spring which could provide the water supply. This meant that the town had no option but to develop southwards, as far as the River Tarn.

On the north and west sides, the monastery wall was part of the town's fortifications. The south side consisted of the church whose main door opened onto what was undoubtedly the main town square. To the east was the abbot's lodging which was extensively rebuilt in the 17th century but which nevertheless has a mediaeval tower; beside it was the Chapel of All the Saints, no longer in existence.

Unfortunately the site was split in half in 1845 by the laying of the Toulouse-Bordeaux railway line. This also led to the demolition of the refectory; the cloister only narrowly escaped the same fate.

On the north side stands the former secondary school, a neo-Gothic building dating from the mid 19th century. The renovation work undertaken there c. 1985, in particular to house a media library and the Marcel-Durliat documentation centre specialising in works on Romanesque architecture revealed the lower section of the mediaeval wall and an entire 13th-century elevation with Gothic arches and twin windows. In fact, very little is known about these secondary buildings in the abbey.

From the hillsides overlooking the valley, the minster can be seen in the foreground. Beyond it is the town, which spread southwards to the River Tarn. (Photo by Guy-Marie Renié)

On the other side of the railway line is the cloister, backing onto the north wall of the church. It was surrounded by the main abbey buildings but they have undergone extensive alteration or been demolished. The numerous alterations, stone or brick work, and re-use of building materials visible here and there bear witness to the age of these walls. The chapter house was on the east side. In the 16th century, it underwent major alteration, as shown by the door leading into the cloister. The monks' refectory, which flanked the north gallery, is known thanks to a few drawings and photographs. As to the west gallery, it flanked a large chapel dedicated to St. Julian. The remains of this chapel have recently been enhanced by the new entrance foyer.

This is where our tour of the abbey begins. By beginning in the cloister, we are undertaking a chronological tour taking us from the late 11th century to the reconstruction of the church in the 15th century.

Visitors arriving from the town may prefer to walk up Rue de la République, slowly approaching the very pinnacle of Romanesque architecture, the South Door.

Late 11th-century bases, colonnettes and capitals were all carefully reassembled between 1260 and 1295. The Gothic arches are built of brick and the square apertures in the squinches lighten the gallery arcading still further. (Photo by Jean-Paul Gisserot)

THE CLOISTER

The cloister in Moissac owes part of its fame to the fact that it is the oldest surviving cloister with narrative capitals. Forty-six of the seventy-six capitals in the four galleries illustrate themes from the Scriptures or depict the lives of the saints. On the pillar in the middle of the west gallery, there is a fine inscription reminding visitors that the cloister, built during the abbacy of Ansquitil (1085-1115) was completed in 1100: ANNO AB INCARNATIONE AETERNI PRINCIPIS MILLESIMO CENTESIMO FACTUM EST CLAUSTRUM ISTUD TEMPORE DOMINI ANSQUITILI ABBATIS AMEN. The text ends with four lines of initials, V.V.V., M.D.R., R.R.R. and F.F.F. Their meaning has never been uncovered.

This is very precise information as to the time at which the cloister was decorated. It is also the period during which reconstruction work began on the abbey church of St. Sernin in Toulouse and the sculptures themselves reflect the contacts between the two sites. When considering the decoration in Moissac, visitors should remember that this is one of the projects which, despite differing artistic temperaments, helped to define Romanesque style at the end of the 11th century.

The arcades in the galleries flanking the vast garth measuring 31 metres (101 ft.) by 27 metres (88 ft.) have alternating single and double colonnettes. This very light structure,

Opposite, right:
West gallery. On the side facing the gallery, the central pillar bears the long inscription indicating that the cloister was completed in 1100 during the abbacy of Ansquitil. The alternating single and double columns imperceptibly soften the unbroken line of the arcades. (Photo by Jean-Paul Gisserot)

Overleaf:
West gallery. From left to right: the Beatitudes (no. 15), corbels of acanthus leaves (no. 14), birds and wild animals (no. 13), rampant foliage (no. 12), the coronation of King David (no. 11) etc. The figurative scenes combine with foliage and animal themes without forming any narrative sequences. (Photo by Guy-Marie Renié)

Capital no. 70. A very serried network of entwined stems and small leaves uniformly covers the entire corbel. The pattern and shallow carving are reminiscent of Moslem ivory carvings which also inspired the pseudo-inscription on the abacus. (Photo by Guy-Marie Renié)

Capital no. 53. The corner scrolls and central dies of the Corinthian capital have been replaced by muzzles spitting out foliage. The plant pattern is laid out around large leaves in a very strict composition. The chamfer of the abacus is decorated with lions and gryphons fighting. (Photo by Guy-Marie Renié)

which supports a simple roof, is strengthened at the corners and in the middle of each side by a masonry pillar.

The cloister has not survived in its original condition. The galleries were rebuilt in the second half of the 13th century, during the abbacy of Bertrand de Montaigut (1260-1295) as is obvious in the Gothic arches in the arcades.

In the north-west corner of the garth stood a fountain whose great marble basin is known only from drawings and descriptions. It was surrounded by arcades identical to the ones in the galleries. They were destroyed before the 19th century but the toothing stones have survived above the central pillar in the north gallery and above the fourth capital in the west gallery.

The capitals are shaped like upturned pyramids, a form which is particularly noticeable in the single capitals. Yet the corbel is structured throughout by the main features inherited from the Corinthian capitals of Ancient Greece, the scrolls facing each other at the corners and the die in the middle of each side. The décor is not limited to corbels. It also covers the abaci at the top of the capitals, providing support for the arches.

Plant decoration was abundant. On a dozen capitals, the foliage is directly inspired by Corinthian capitals (e.g. no. 54). They have deeply indented acanthus leaves with shapes very similar to the ones seen on the galleries in St. Sernin's Basilica.

Other corbels are covered with wreaths of foliage superimposed on the rough-hewn stone without changing its texture. The serried leaves unfurl in the same, deep, hollow plane (no. 41) and were probably inspired by Moslem ivory carvings, while the flexible stems enclosing the beautiful palmettes and pine cones (no. 51) are reminiscent of a motif that was widely used in the second half of the 11th century throughout the south-west of France and north-west of Spain.

Although some of the corbels com-

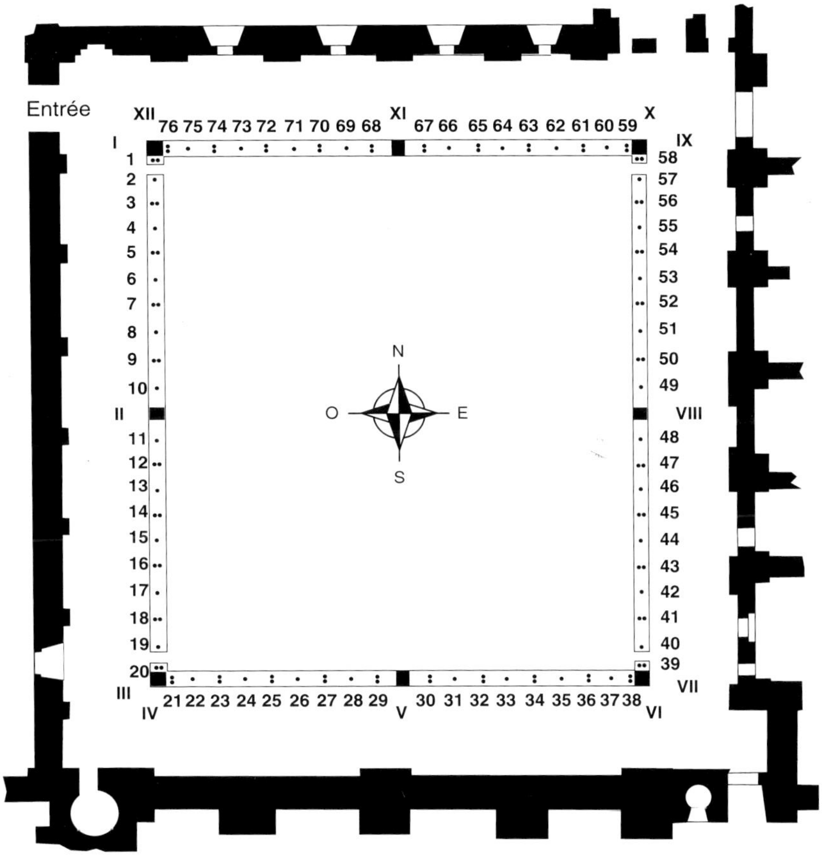

Plan : Quitterie Cazes

West gallery

I. ST. PHILIP

1. Abraham's sacrifice
Palmette frieze

2. Glorification of the Cross
Monsters

3. Acanthus leaves
Flower frieze

4. Birds in combat
Pairs of lions

5. Daniel in the lions' den; the Good Tidings brought to the shepherds
Palmette frieze

6. Acanthus leaves
Fruit garland

7. Monsters with trunks and bows
Foliage

8. Resurrection of Lazarus
Frieze of cruciform flowers

9. Palms
Palmette frieze

10. Imaginary characters and animals
Stems entwining roses and interlaced snakes

II. ST. SIMON. Inscription

11. Coronation of David by the prophet Samuel
Palmette frieze

12. Rampant plant decoration
Entwined stems

13. Birds and wild animals
Friezes and palmettes

14. Acanthus leaves
Palmette frieze

15. The Beatitudes
Foliage entwining leaves and two heads

16. Lions in combat and human faces
Stylised plant décor

17. Story of Cain and Abel
Stems entwining rosettes

18. Rampant plant décor
Entwined stems

19. Ascension of Alexander?
Medallions held by two angels, containing a head

20. David and Goliath
Palmette frieze

III. ST. BARTHOLOMEW

South gallery

IV. ST. MATTHEW

21. Herod's Feast and the Beheading of St. John the Baptist
Palmette frieze

22. Birds in tree-like plants
Frieze of two-headed eagles

23. The City of Babylon
Foliage entwining leaves

24. Birds in combat
Heads of animals spitting out interlaces

25. Nebuchadnezzar's Dream
Palmette frieze. Inscription

26. Martyrdom of St. Stephen
Stylised foliage and balls

27. Acanthus leaves
Lions

28. David and the angel musicians
Imaginary birds and animals

29. The City of Jerusalem
Palmette frieze

30. The well of the abyss
Foliage entwining leaves

31. Symbols of the Evangelists
Wild animals fighting

32. Woman of Canaan and the centurion
Stylised foliage and balls

33. Good Samaritan
Animals and people in foliage. Inscription

34. Temptation of Christ
Palmette frieze

35. Vision of St. John on Patmos
Interlaced animals grasping horned heads

36. The Transfiguration of Christ
Plant frieze

37. St. Peter's imprisonment and release
A frieze of devils, inspired by Kufic script

38. Baptism of Christ
Palmette frieze

VI. ST. PAUL

East gallery

VII. ST. PETER

39. Samson and the lion of Gabatta
Palmette frieze

40. Martyrdom of St. Peter and St. Paul
Foliage entwining leaves. Inscription

41. Rampant plant décor
Stems entwining roses. Alphabet

42. Original sin
Foliage entwining leaves.

43. Acanthus leaves
Stylised plant decoration

44. Martyrdom of St. Lawrence?
Lions, gryphons, goat and ram

45. Christ washing the disciples' feet
Mandorla held by two angels, containing the hand of God or a head

46. Palms
Birds fighting in foliage

47. Lazarus and the rich man
Frieze of cherubs. Inscription

48. Gryphons fighting and grasping heads in their claws
Foliage

VIII. DURAND DE BREDONS

49. Figures seizing eagles by the neck
Stylised plant décor

50. Marriage in Cana
Palmette frieze

51. Rampant plant decoration and pinecones
Stems entwining roses

52. Adoration of the Magi; Massacre of the Holy Innocents
Foliage

53. Foliage and nuzzles
Lions and gryphons

54. Acanthus leaves
Palmette frieze

55. Martyrdom of St. Saturnin
Palmette frieze

56. Acanthus leaves
Palmette frieze

57. Martyrdom of St. Fructueux, St. Augure and St. Euloge
Palmette frieze

58. Annunciation and Visitation of Mary
Palmette frieze

IX.ST. JAMES

North gallery

X. ST. JOHN

59. Angels slaying dragons
Palmette frieze

60. Eagles
Pairs of fish

61. Rampant plant decoration
Lions, gryphons, ram and goat

62. Two miracles of St. Benedict
Foliage around leaves. Inscription

63. Imaginary birds fighting
Birds fighting in foliage

64. St. Peter healing a paralysed man
Palmette frieze

65. Rampant plant decoration
Interlaced birds, stags and horses fighting

66. Celestial Court
Palmette frieze

67. Miraculous catch
Dragons

68. Daniel in the lions' den and Habakkuk the prophet
People and animals fighting

69. Arrival of the Crusaders in Jerusalem?
Stems entwining roses and a dove

70. Rampant plant decoration
Foliage entwining leaves. Inscription in fake Kufic script

71. Symbols of the Evangelists
Stylised plant decoration

72. Birds fighting
Birds interlaced

73. Three young Hebrews in the fiery furnace
Mandorla held by angels, containing the hand of God, the Lamb of God, the head of Christ or the Dove

74. Story of St. Martin
Animals and gryphons. Inscription

75. Rampant plant decoration
Palmette frieze

76. Jesus and the woman of Samaria
Palmette frieze

XII. ST. ANDREW

Capital no. 40. The martyrdom of St. Peter and St. Paul, identified by the inscription on the abacus. A small cavity on the side facing the gallery used to contain their relics. St. Peter was crucified head downwards, at his own request since he considered himself unworthy to be crucified in the same way as Christ. (Photo by Guy-Marie Renié)

bine plants and animals, there are several examples of eagles and lions depicted on their own. Animal motifs, though, are most frequent on the abaci where they take the form of real or imaginary animals depicted in strips or engaged in battle. Some of them also include human faces. The narrow strip at the top of the abacus allows for nothing more than a scant geometric pattern, scales or stone insets. One of them contains an inscription in fake Kufic script (no. 70) which may have been copied from an ivory carving or piece of fabric imported from a Moslem country.

Some of the abaci also bear inscriptions relating to the pictorial elements on the capital beneath. This proves how carefully the re-assembly work was carried out in the 13th century. On the capital depicting the life of St. Martin (no. 74), the text provides a commentary, «Martin, while still a catechumen, gave a pauper half of his cloak. Christ then appeared to him, wearing the garment. When a bishop, he raised a novice from the dead (MARTINUS ADHUC CATEHCUMANUS HAC ME VESTE CONTEXIT HIS MARTINUS ELECTUS DEI PONTIFEX). Another capital depicts the parable of the Good Samaritan (no. 33) who took care of a traveller wounded by thieves and left untended at the roadside by a priest and a Levite (ET INCIDIT IN LATRONES SAMARITANUS QUIDAM SACERDOTES CUM LEVITA PERTRANSIIT CURAM ILLIUS HABE).

In Moissac, it is impossible not to be struck by the sheer number of inscriptions that accompany the carvings, whether mere identifications of the figures or comments on the themes depicted. The importance placed on them should be considered in the light of the wealth and precision of the subject matter often depicted for the very first time in the highly restrictive framework of a capital.

The amount of narrative decoration in the cloister galleries was doubtless stimulated by the fact that they were there, visible to all, offering the monks subjects for meditation. There is no continuous narrative; instead the scenes invite people seeing them to confirm their faith in Divine Love.

Eleven capitals carry themes from the Old Testament, reinterpreted in the light of the Gospels. They include the Fall of Adam and Eve (no. 42), a reminder of Original Sin stamped upon humanity, Abraham's Sacrifice (no. 1) showing him ready to cut his son's throat and the son being replaced by a ram, or carvings of Samson (no. 39) or David (nos. 28, 11) which have become figures of Christ.

Even more of the capitals represent the life or teachings of Christ i.e. the Annunciation (no. 58), the Adoration of the Magi (no. 52), the Beheading of St. John the Baptist (no. 21), the Miraculous Catch (no. 67), the Washing of the Feet (no. 45) the parable of Lazarus and the Rich Man (no. 47) or the Beatitudes (no. 15). Strangely, there is no carving of the Crucifixion.

Three capitals represent St. Peter (nos. 37, 64 and 40). His martyrdom is combined with that of St. Paul. There are four illustrating the Vision of St. John (nos. 35, 29, 23 and 30). Next to the martyrdom of St. Stephen (no. 26) and St. Lawrence (no. 44) are those of the first bishops of Toulouse and Tarragon, Saturnin (no. 55) and Fructueux (no. 57). The obligation to provide charity is recalled again with St. Martin's sharing of his cloak (no. 74). St. Martin and St. Benedict (no. 62) are shown working miracles in God's name – hardly surprising in a Benedictine monastery.

Each capital is worth a long, studious look for its subject matter and its carving, with total disregard for the almost total mutilation of the faces.

After the capitals, the carvings on the pillars are among the finest examples of Romanesque artistry. Nine of the Apostles are represented and identified by name. It is possible that the remaining three were depicted on the portico surrounding the fountain. The purpose of the carvings was to indicate that the original monastic ideal was to be seen in the Apostles and, with little hesitation, the first Cluniac Abbot of Moissac was added to the group. Durand de Bredons, Abbot of Moissac and Bishop of Toulouse, bearing a halo because he was acknowledged as a saint shortly after his death, once stood on the central

Capital no. 38. The Baptism of Christ. Jesus waded into the River Jordan until the water reached His waist then received baptism from St. John the Baptist while the dove of the Holy Spirit descended on Him. Two apostles are bringing him clothes. On the side panels, an angel brandishes a book and another a Cross. (Photo by Guy-Marie Renié)

Capital no. 55. The Martyrdom of St. Saturnin. The story of the martyrdom of the first Bishop of Toulouse is told on four sides. He is shown, tied to the bull which he refused to sacrifice to honour the pagan gods, as his skull is smashed against the steps of the Capitole temple. (Photo by Guy-Marie Renié)

pillar of the east gallery, opposite the entrance to the chapter house.

The works are striking for their graphic quality. The very shallow carving is well suited to the thin slabs of marble, all of them taken from the bases of sarcophagi. Some of them were re-used whole. They are reminiscent of the illuminations on manuscripts and, again, carvings in ivory. The same theme, great figures beneath arches, was being used at almost the same time in St. Sernin's Basilica in Toulouse although Bernard Gilduin used sculpture for a very different purpose, seeking to accentuate relief in models that were Roman in inspiration.

Unfortunately the cloister in Moissac has lost most of the buildings that once flanked it. They were either demolished or extensively altered.

In the rooms laid out within the chapter house on the east side are a number of furnishings and a small quantity of church plate, including a glove plate and a gold pastoral ring dating from c. 1300.

The chapel dedicated to St. Ferréol, located in the north-east corner, and the small room adjacent to it on the west side still have their mediaeval structure. They now contain the abbey's archaeological museum and include the capitals that were no doubt part of the late 11th-century chapter house. Other capitals come from the arcading round the fountain. Among the sculptures removed during the restoration of the doorway are two fragments of the Angel of the Annunciation.

A small door in the south-west corner of the cloister takes visitors to the spiral staircase leading up to the chamber in the westwork and its crenelated curtain walls.

The statue of Durand de Bredons, the first Cluniac Abbot of Moissac and Bishop of Toulouse, stands opposite the door to the chapter house. Carved in thin marble plaques taken from ancient sarcophagi, the sculptures on the pillar show particular graphic skill. (Photo by Guy-Marie Renié)

THE WESTWORK AND DOORWAY

Thanks to Marcel Durliat, the circumstances surrounding the construction of the westwork are now more fully understood. It was the subject of a court case that opposed Abbot Roger (1115-c. 1135) to the "Abbot-Knight" Bertrand de Montancès. During a hearing in Toulouse in May 1130, Count Alphonse-Jourdain was forced to recognise his injustice towards the abbey some time earlier. He handed down a ruling confirming that the church and the existing or subsequent bell towers were under the sole authority of the abbot and his successors. This meant that the tower on the westwork became a symbol of the independence and spiritual, economic and political might of Cluny Abbey.

It was a sturdy construction, similar to the west tower in Saint-Benoît-sur-Loire, with a chapel above the porch serving as an entrance to the church. Its current condition is due to the restoration undertaken in the 1850's by Viollet-le-Duc who rebuilt the battlements from a few merlons that still existed, without modifying the upper section of the brick bell tower dating from the 15th and 17th centuries.

Once the work on the cloister was finished, Abbot Ansquitil is said to have launched this part of the building project in 1110-1115. The first storey was already erected when the initial project was modified and the tower included in thick walls apparently designed as part of the system of defence. This change of plan is obvious on the west elevation where the great arch partially blocks the upper bays in the early construction. On the south side, the doorway was preceded by a deep embrasure in the impressive wall topped by two rows of crenelations. Two half-columns bearing effigies of two monks flank the entrance. At the top of the half-column on the right is Abbot Roger who had died a short time earlier and who is described as "Blessed" in the identifying inscription.

The westwork is topped by crenelations, giving it a fortified appearance. The battlements were rebuilt by Viollet-le-Duc in the 1850's. The 15th-century brick bell tower is topped by a double pediment that was added in the 17th century. (Photo by Guy-Marie Renié)

Overleaf:
Tympanum. In the centre of the doorway is St. John's Vision of the Apocalypse. The Christ-God appears enthroned between the four Beasts, a seraphim and a cherubim, and the twenty-four Elders singing His praises. The layout in rows, which is reminiscent of the layout of the tympanum on the north door of the cathedral in Cahors, fades as the eye is drawn to the space containing the figure of Christ. (Photo by Guy-Marie Renié)

Set in a deep splay, the doorway displays a coherent iconography. Around the Glorious Return of Christ and the Last Judgement represented on the tympanum are the Old and New Laws, the Incarnation of the Saviour and the fate reserved for the Just

To the right of the doorway is the figure of Abbot Roger (1115-c. 1135) who commissioned the building of the westwork and, probably, the decorative carvings. (Photo by Guy-Marie Renié)

This means that the decoration on the South Door, with the masterpiece that is the tympanum, dates from 1115-1130. Some twenty years, scarcely one generation, separate this from the carvings in the cloister. It is easy to appreciate the stylistic development achieved thanks to the driving force of an artistic genius such as the creator of the doorway in Moissac.

The **tympanum** is directly inspired by the Book of Revelations, written by St. John:

"After this I looked and, behold, a door was opened in heaven... and, behold, a throne was set in heaven, and one sat on the throne... And round about the throne were four and twenty seats: and upon the seats I saw four and twenty elders sitting, clothed in white raiment: and they had on their heads crowns of gold. And out of the throne proceeded lightnings and thunderings and voices... And before the throne there was a sea of glass like unto crystal... and round about the throne were four beasts... And the first beast was like a lion, and the second beast like a calf, and the third beast had a face as a man, and the fourth beast was like a flying eagle... and they rest not day and night, saying, Holy, holy, holy, Lord God Almighty, which was, and is, and is to come...And I saw in the right hand of him that sat on the throne a book... sealed with seven seals... And I beheld... a Lamb... And he came and took the book... And when he had taken the book, the four beasts and four and twenty-elders fell down before the Lamb, having every one of them harps, and golden vials full of odours, which are the prayers of saints. And they sung a new song, saying "Thou art worthy to take the book, and to open the seals thereof; for thou wast slain, and hast redeemed us to God by thy blood out of every kindred, and tongue, and people, and nation."

Close-up of the tympanum. The Christ-God, the Beginning and the End, occupies the entire central section of the tympanum on which figures are represented in a size proportionate to their importance. The symbolism of the entrance is further enriched by the allegory to which Christ refers in the parable of the Good Shepherd, "I am the door: by me if any man enter in, he shall be saved". (John 10, v.9) (Photo by Guy-Marie Renié)

Close-up of the tympanum. Three of the Elders (or kings) on the second row. The sculptor has tried to vary attitudes and clothes on the twenty-four people without destroying the overall unity. His style is evident in the ease of movement and in the vigorous way in which the clothing falls over the legs. (Photo by Guy-Marie Renié)

In the 2nd century, the four beasts were identified as the four Evangelists and represented holding a book. St. Matthew was an angel, St. Mark a lion, St. Luke a bull and St. John an eagle. Two seraphim flank Christ, one holding a closed roll of parchment, the other with an open phylactery. The Last Judgement is approaching, the day on which all that is written will be accomplished, when each shall be judged according to his works and where he whose name is not written in the Book of Life shall be rejected.

Christ in Glory sits in majestic immobility in the centre of two tumultuous circles formed by the Beasts and angels then the twenty-four kings. The differences in attitude add weight to the sheer number of figures creating a crowd that nevertheless directs the gaze perfectly, leading it towards the contemplation of God. The sculptor has succeeded in pushing the strict layout imposed by the form of the tympanum into the background. The same stylistic achievement led him to place in the upper section the folded ribbon which would otherwise have highlighted the framework imposed by the architecture.

The richness of the folds and orphreys (the gemstone edgings used to decorate clothes) should not give a misleadingly precious impression of the art. In fact, the movements are depicted with vigour, as are the details in the clothing, overlaying or imbricated in the line and fall of the cloth.

The supernatural character of Christ's apparition, in Glory, is further emphasised by the superb row of roses running right the way across the lintel built of three blocks of re-used marble. Beneath, the scrolls of vine and acanthus have been left visible. The decoration is similar to that of 4th-5th century sarcophagi. The roses are perfect replicas of the ones decorating the Palaeo-Christian lintel discovered in St. Sernin's church in Thézels and now displayed in the museum in Cahors. The motif is used again on the pier as a base for the pairs of crossed lions and lionesses that support the lintel and guard the entrance to the church.

Entrance, left side of the splay. The first two rows beneath the arches illustrate the themes of Avarice and Lewdness. In contrast, the upper row shows the fate of Lazarus the pauper, dying at the rich man's door. His soul is taken into the bosom of Abraham. To the left is St. Luke pointing to the text of his gospel. (Photo by Jean-Paul Gisserot)

The tympanum depicts only the Vision of the Apocalypse. The lower sections of the doorway are coherently decorated with subjects depicting the Incarnation of Christ and the promise of Judgement.

The Old and New Laws are represented on the sides of the pier by the very fine figures of Jeremiah (right) and St. Paul (left). This was an opportunity for the sculptor to produce individualised faces, contrasting the severity of St. Paul and the melancholic gentleness of Jeremiah. The bodies back onto a column which is scarcely visible in the background, stretching immoderately upwards across the narrow surface of the support.

Opposite St. Paul, on the jamb, is St. Peter stamping on a devil; opposite Jeremiah is the prophet Isaiah with a phylactery announcing that a virgin will have a child: ECCE VIRGO CONCIPIET.

It is the childhood of Christ which is depicted in the carvings on the right side of the splay. Beneath arcading are statues representing the Annunciation (the angel was recarved in the 19th century) and the Visitation (two polyester moulds replace the sculptures which have required special treatment in order to conserve them); above them is the Adoration of the Magi. The upper section includes the Presentation in the Temple (right) then the Flight into Egypt where idols fall to dust as the Virgin Mary and Her son arrive.

The left side of the splay illustrates the fate reserved for each one of us, depending on our acts and actions. On the top string-course, the wealthy man and his wife are sitting at table, deaf to the complaints of Lazarus the pauper whose dogs are licking his ulcers. His soul (all that remains are the feet of the tiny body symbolising it) is being lifted upwards by an angel and taken to Abraham while St. Luke points to the text in his gospel. Beneath the arches is the wealthy man on his deathbed, with his weeping wife. His soul is being carried away by demons to suffer the torments of Hell (*left*). Beneath is the Miser with a huge purse round his neck, possessed by the Devil and refusing to give alms to a beggar. The panel on the right depicts lewdness in all its horror.

Pier on the left side of the entrance. St. Paul is shown as being bald, in accordance with a tradition that was already well-established. He has a severe expression on his face. With St. Peter, he represents the New Law. He stands opposite Jeremiah and Isaiah who announced the New Alliance. (Photo by Guy-Marie Renié)

Pier on the right side of the entrance. Like the statue of St. Paul, Jeremiah backs onto a column. The capital consisting of two large fluted leaves can be seen above the head of the statue. The gentleness of the carving and of Jeremiah's expression makes this one of the best known sculptures in Moissac. (Photo by Jean-Paul Gisserot)

On the central capital of the arches, the souls of the damned burn in eternal flames stoked by a demon with a pair of bellows.

The aesthetic quality of the architecture and sculpture reflects the religious thought behind it. From both points of view, Moissac can be considered as one of the most consummate examples of a narrative doorway and one of the great masterpieces of Romanesque architecture.

Archaeological digs carried out in 1985 revealed the Romanesque tread in the entrance. After restoration, the doorway has now regained its original proportions. Visitors climb a few steps into the vast porch which precedes the nave of the church.

The vault is supported by two huge diagonal arches. The decoration is restricted almost entirely to the huge capitals topping massive half-columns – stags' heads above a crown of crossettes, interlaced stems bearing large grainy fruit, animal mouths spitting out palmettes, pairs of wolves and she-wolves carrying away lambs etc. The particularly fine style of the carving of Samson slaying a lion is recognisable as belonging to the sculptor responsible for the doorway.

The **upper chamber** is amazing for its architecture. The square is roofed with twelve cells supported on thick rectangular ribs radiating out from a ringed keystone. This room, as we have said, is accessible from the cloister.

Opposite:
Entrance, right side of the splay. The upper row shows a narrative sequence depicting the Childhood of Christ in a manner that is quite picturesque. From right to left, the Presentation in the Temple, the Flight into Egypt and the fall of the idols after the arrival of the Virgin Mary and Infant Jesus. (Photo by Guy-Marie Renié)

Below:
Entrance, right side of the splay. The Adoration of the Magi occupies the entire middle section above the Annunciation and the Visitation. The Three Kings are advancing towards the Child indicated by the star. Behind Mary, still lying in bed, stands Joseph. (Photo by Guy-Marie Renié)

A capital in the porch. The theme of Samson slaying the lion is repeated symmetrically. The style of the capitals in the porch is indicative of the artistry displayed by the sculptor who carved the entrance. (Photo by Jean-Paul Gisserot)

Opposite, right:
The upper chapel in the westwork. The vaulting is supported on twelve square ribs radiating out from a circular keystone. (Photo by Jean-Paul Gisserot)

Opposite, left:
The porch. Four sturdy square ribs were used to vault this vast space preceding the nave. The doorway into the nave has trefoil arches which were rebuilt in 1920 over surviving bases. (Photo by Jean-Paul Gisserot)

Nave of the church, view towards the chancel. During the reconstruction in the 15th century, the interior of the nave, which still has some Romanesque features in the first three bays, was brought greater unity by the use of a geometrical pattern on the walls. (Photo by Jean-Paul Gisserot)

THE CHURCH

After the dimness in the mighty porch, visitors discover a brightly-lit nave in the Gothic style developed in the south of France. The side chapels laid out between the piers do not alter the sheer volume of the single aisle, which leads into a polygonal apse of the same width. The ribbed vaulting rises to a constant height of 22 metres (72 ft.) and is supported in the nave by a frieze of thorny foliage. The work was taken up again by Abbot Aymeric de Roquemaurel (1431-1449) who had the apse and first three bays at the eastern end of the nave rebuilt. The work was not finished until the days of Abbots Pierre and Antoine de Carmaing (1449-1501) whose arms decorate the keystones in the bays at the west end.

The general sense of uniformity is strengthened by the painted decoration consisting solely of repetitive geometric motifs in warm, light colours. The restoration work finished in 1964 gave the church back the appearance it had until the 18th century. However, this is only a surface uniformity. In the four bays at the west end, the thick walls on the lower level date from the Romanesque church. To build the intersecting ribs, the two original wide bays had to be divided by pillars which obstructed the middle windows. An analysis of the work is much easier from the outside where the pier built against the Romanesque window and the freestone elevation set in the brick wall from the Gothic period are much more visible. The nave should be imagined like the one in St. Stephen's Cathedral in Cahors built in the first half of the 12th century. Each square bay roofed by a vast dome on pendentives is lit by two rows of three rounded windows. This, at least, was the project launched in the mid 12th century, no doubt shortly after the completion of the westwork. There is no doubt that the first bay dates from this period. The second bay, however, was built after the end of the 13th century as is evident from the prism-shaped bases and naturalistic foliage of the windows. The work probably stopped there and the eastern section of the church built in 1063 was probably retained until the 15th century.

Furnishings

A 4th- or 5th- century **sarcophagus** was re-used to build the tomb of Abbot Raymond de Montpezat who died a saintly death in 1245 and was much venerated in the 14th century by the afflicted. They would stand under the tomb and pray for a return to health. The tomb rests on two large marble capitals dating from the end of the Roman period. Above the deeply trepanned acanthus leaves are two doves drinking out of a cantharus. The sarcophagus is a typical example of the ones made of Pyrenean marble. In panels separated by pilasters or simple moulding, there are shallow carvings of tree acanthus and scrolls of vines or ivy. A central medallion contains Christ's monogram represented by the chrism of Constantinople flanked by the letters alpha and omega. Below is a carving frequently used in Palaeo-Christian art showing doves drinking from a cantharus.

The wonderful **Romanesque statue** of the crucified Christ, made of painted wood, was placed on a Cross with arms reminiscent of a Tree of Life, perhaps in the 13th century. The truncated stems rising from the foot of the Cross were still topped by two angels in the 17th century. A study by Willibald Sauerländer gave a new vision of this figure of Christ which can now be attributed to the sculptor who carved the doorway in the period between 1115 and 1130. It includes the same long strands of hair as those of the Elders on the tympanum or of the lecherous woman, the characteristic positioning of the ears rather high up on the head, and the same vigorous cuts marking the folds of the perizonium or the naked body of Christ. It is quite exceptional to be able to compare two 12th-century works that are so different in function and material.

Arches in the nave, highlighted by the painted decoration. They are supported on capital-friezes with deeply carved foliage in a style undoubtedly of the 15th century. (Photo by Guy-Marie Renié)

A close-up of the Romanesque Crucifix made of painted wood. The rather unusual Cross, on which the arms are reminiscent of the Tree of Life, is probably post 13th century. The style of the figure of Christ is such that it has been attributed to the sculptor who carved the doorway in 1115-1130. (Photo by Guy-Marie Renié)

The period of revival in the 15th century was marked by the carving of a number of fine group sculptures.

The statues of St. John the Evangelist and Mary Magdalen flank a **Pietà**. Below, featured in miniature, are the donors (the head of the figure on the left has been recarved) identified by an inscription on the base: *Moncen J. de la Gariga. Goussen de la Gariga / l'an mil CCCC LXXVI me firent fere les de sus dit* (My Lord J. de la Gariga, Goussen de la Gariga / in the year one thousand four hundred and seventy-six had me make the aforenamed). Even if the apostle was not named he would have been easily recognisable for his young face. Mary Magdalen, the repentant sinner whose long hair is straggling out from underneath her veil, exhorts those who pass by, *"Non desperetis vos qui peccare soletis, exemploque meo vos reparate Deo"* (Do not despair, you who are accustomed to sin, and through my example move closer to God!). Given the strength of the carving, it would be churlish to describe a certain clumsiness in the over-short proportions or the rigid, conventional attitude. Instead, those who see the statue are overwhelmed by the beauty of the folds in the clothing and the sadness in the faces.

The group representing the **Flight into Egypt** consists of a Madonna and Child on a small donkey (late 15th century) and a figure of St. Joseph that was recarved in the 17th. The very different treatment of the clothes, faces and hair leave no doubt in this respect. This anecdotal scene is an opportunity to illustrate the tenderness between a young woman and her child, represented with the rather stilted grace that often marks late mediaeval art. Mathieu Méras attributed this work to the craftsmen who produced the Entombment.

As visitors enter the chapel now containing the **Entombment**, they are confronted by a seemingly living tableau, as their mediaeval forebears

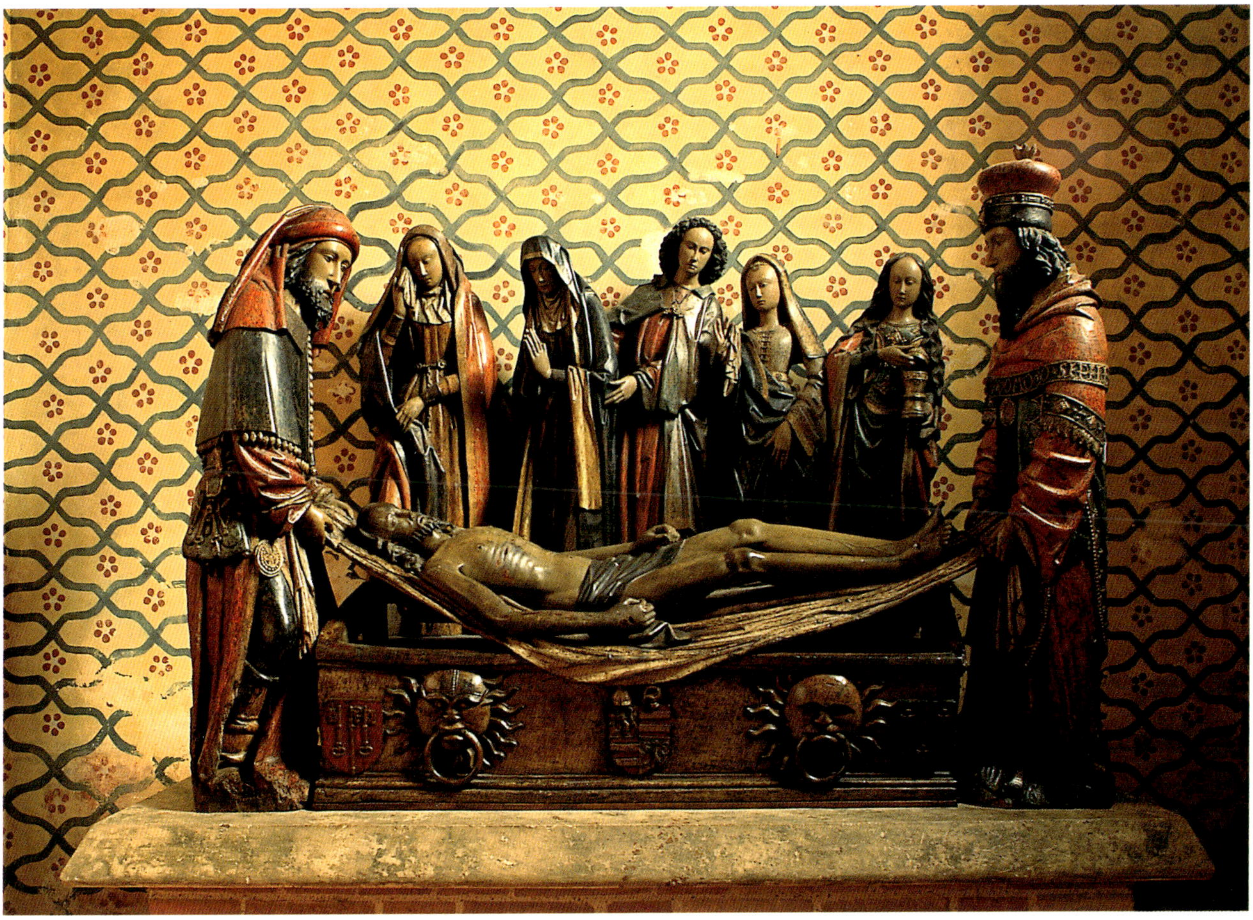

Entombment, c. 1500. This large painted wooden group statue stood in the Chapel of All the Saints until the end of the 18th century. The chapel was the last resting-place of the abbots. (Photo by Guy-Marie Renié)

were in the days of the mystery plays. Seven life-sized statues are burying the dead Christ. St. John is supporting the Virgin Mary who is praying, Her eyes fixed on the face of Her Son. They are surrounded by the three Mary's – Mary Salome, Mary of Cleophas and Mary Magdalen carrying a pot of balm, her long hair flowing free. Joseph of Arimathea (left) and Nicodaemus (right) are slowly laying the body in a sarcophagus. The commentary for the scene is spelt out round the hem of Nicodaemus' robe: ECCO QUOMODO SEPELITUR JUSTUS (This is how the Just was buried).

The style dates from the 1500's and this has led to the supposition that Abbot Antoine de Carmaing was responsible for the commission. His family crest decorates the centre of the sarcophagus while the coat-of-arms of the abbey is represented to the left.

At the end of the 18th century, the group included twelve figures and was placed in a small chapel which no longer exists. It was dedicated to All the Saints and was the burial place of the abbots. Restoration work undertaken in 1956 enabled the various figures to be repositioned and the original paintwork was rediscovered.

The **choirscreen** is a fine piece of work from the First Renaissance period, dated by Anthony Blunt as c. 1520. Only a small section has survived. The wings were removed and two sections re-used for the side doors. All that remained before it was totally cleaned in the 19th century was the element surrounding the altar. Only imagination can recreate the stone screen, which may have been painted and gilded and which jutted out into the nave and connected the monks' choirstalls. The High Altar is a strange construction with an upper platform bearing an altar dedicated to St. Michael. The fluted columns, pilasters, entablatures, tympani and traceried balustrades reveal in-depth knowledge of Italian altars.

Through the screen in the left door of the enclosure, it is possible to see, set into the wall of the apse, the inscription commemorating the consecration of the church on the eighth day

Pietà, St. John and St. Mary Magdalen. The painted stone group statue was probably a votive offering, gifted in 1476 by townsmen of Moissac who were appointed Consuls between 1473 and 1489. (Photo by Guy-Marie Renié)

The Flight into Egypt (painted wood). The statue of St. Joseph is 17th century while the Madonna and Child on the donkey comes from a 15th-century group statue, perhaps by the same sculptor who carved the Entombment. (Photo by Guy-Marie Renié)

of the Ides of November (6th November) 1063. It names the eight bishops who attended the ceremony and specifies that the Bishop of Cahors was not permitted to join them (as a result of quarrels over precedence). It then recalls that the monastery founded by Clovis received gifts and donations from Louis the Pious.

Before leaving the church, enter the Chapel of the Holy Sacrament. A small, moving 15th-century Pietà is mounted against the east wall. It is unusually compact in design. There is another unexpected feature at the back of a low window in the west wall – a small stained-glass window by Marc Chagall, a gift from the artist himself in 1972. A bouquet of flowers in a vase and the face of a young woman are drawn, in grisaille, on a background of white, pink and yellow glass.

From the square outside, study the church in its entirety. It is easy to distinguish the various periods of construction – westwork, Romanesque nave and 15th-century reconstruction.

It would be a pity not to extend the visit just that bit longer. Walk along the outside of the nave and round the east end to the abbot's lodging which houses the collections in the Musée Marguerite-Vidal, mainly furniture and objects from the Lower Quercy area. The tower flanking 17th-century apartments was built over an 11th-century chapel and the vaulting still has traces of painting dating from c. 1200. Still visible are the scrolls of foliage and the figures on a Rod of Jesse.

On the other side of the railway line are the buildings in the former secondary school, now the media library and the Marcel Durliat Centre for Romanesque Art and Architecture (*centre d'art roman Marcel-Durliat*).

The choirscreen, c. 1520. This is a fine Renaissance work which shows deep understanding of the Italian style. The altarscreen is built into a strange construction supporting an altar dedicated to St. Michael and overlooking the chancel. (Photo by Guy-Marie Renié)

Bibliography

Ernest Rupin, *L'abbaye et les cloîtres de Moissac*, 1897, réédité par les Ed. Les Monédières, 1981.

Marguerite Vidal, Jean Maury, Jean Porcher, *Quercy roman*, La-Pierre-qui-Vire, 1959 (coll. *Zodiaque*).

Marcel Durliat, *L'abbaye de Moissac*, Rennes, Ouest-France, 1985.

Maurice Scellès, Marie-Anne Sire, Evelyne Ugaglia, *La ville de Moissac*, Toulouse, APAMP, 1986.

Marcel Durliat, *La sculpture romane de la route de Saint-Jacques. De Conques à Compostelle*, Mont-de-Marsan, CEHAG, 1990.

Maurice Scellès, Quitterie Cazes, *Le cloître de Moissac, chef-d'œuvre de la sculpture romane*, Bordeaux, Éditions Sud Ouest, 2001.

Tourist Office: Tel. (0) 563 040 185. **Cloister:** open daily except Christmas Day and New Year's Day, 9 a.m. to noon and 2 p.m. to 6 p.m. 1st July to 31st August, open 9 a.m. to 7 p.m. (later on Friday evenings). Guided tours in July and August or by prior arrangement all year. **Centre d'art roman Marcel-Durliat:** Tel. (0) 563 044 179.

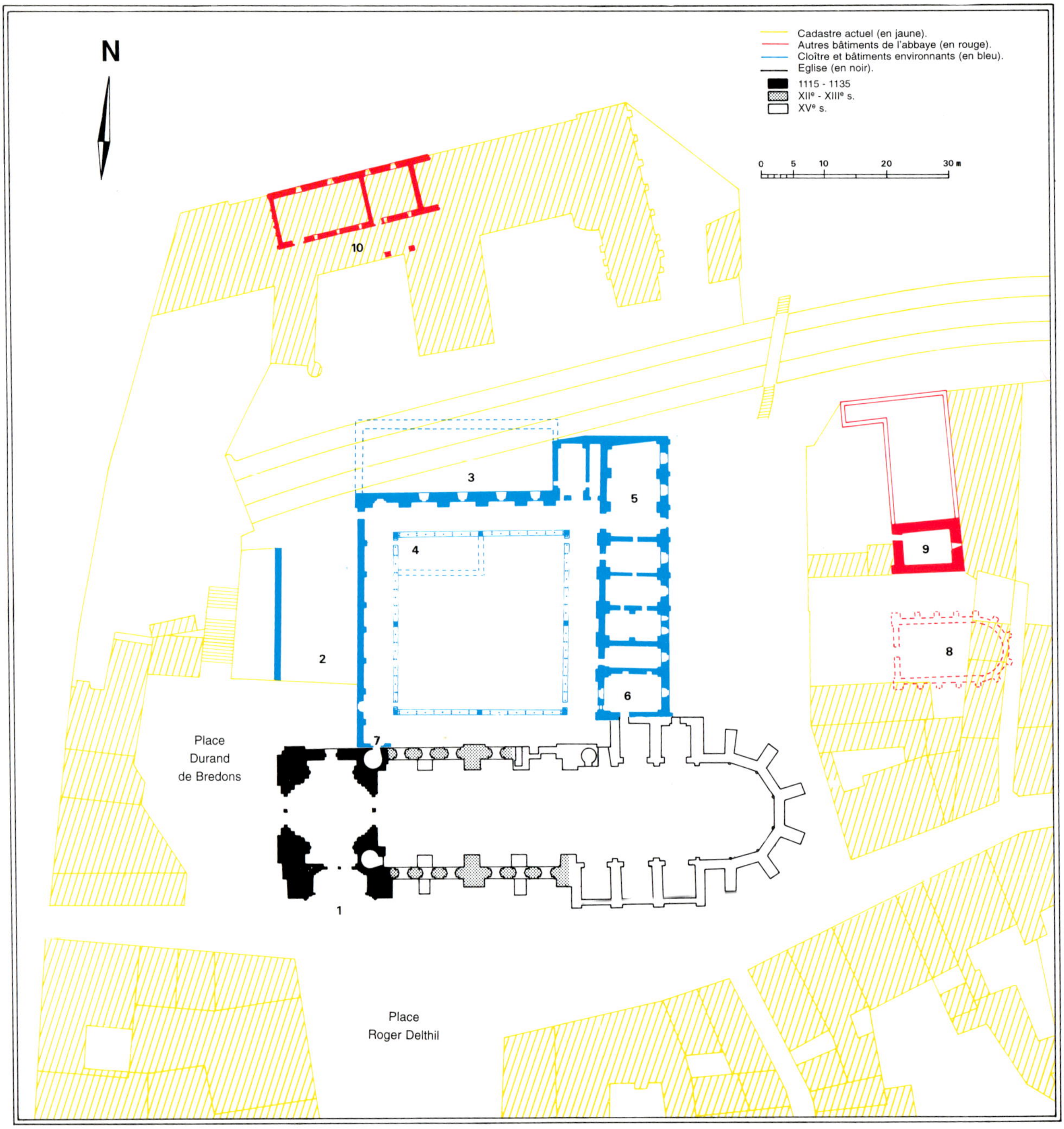

Plan : Maurice Scellès

1. Romanesque doorway
2. Remains of St. Julian's Chapel, now the entrance foyer
3. Refectory (no longer in existence)
4. Site of the fountain
5. St. Ferréol's Chapel
6. Chapel of the Holy Sacrament
7. Staircase to the upper storey in the westwork
8. Supposed site of the Chapel of All the Saints
9. 11th-century chapel in the abbot's lodging
10. Remains of the north buildings

Front cover : Close-up of the prophet Jeremiah, carved on the right side of the pier in the entrance.

Back cover : Nave of the church; A close-up of the Romanesque Crucifix; Capital no. 53.

 Ce livre a été imprimé par Pollina à Luçon (85) - France.
ISBN : 2.87901.387.9 - Editeur : 1021.02.02.04.05 - N° d'impression : 96461B